About the author

I was born in Eritrea. In 2014 I fled my homeland to escape the inhuman regime of the military dictatorship. I have successfully completed secondary school in my home country. In 2017 my stay in Germany was approved. I learned German and got my German school-leaving certificate. Today I live in Hanover and have successfully completed further training as an IT system administrator in healthcare/DHSE.

Russom Teklay

Triumphing Throug Adversity
The
Journey to Success

CONTENTS

Chapter 1
Embracing Challenges:
The Path to Triumph

Welcome to the first chapter of our journey to success! In life, we encounter a myriad of challenges that often make us feel like we're in an obstacle course. But hey, that's what makes life exciting and worthwhile, right? So, let's dive into the wonderful world of embracing challenges and discover how it can lead us to a life of triumph and success!

The Nature of Challenges:
Life has a funny way of throwing curveballs our way just when we think we've got it all figured out. Challenges come in a variety of forms - personal, professional, health-related, or even societal pressures. It's easy to view these challenges as roadblocks, but what if we tried looking at them as opportunities for growth and learning?

Think about it - when you face a challenge, you're presented with an opportunity to test your skills, push your boundaries, and rise above the situation. Embracing challenges means recognizing that they're an essential part of the human experience and that each one carries the potential for something amazing to unfold.

The Growth Mindset:
Let's talk about the "growth mindset". It's like having a magical pair of glasses that lets you see challenges in a whole new light. When you wear these glasses, you understand that your abilities and intelligence are not fixed traits. Instead, they can be developed through dedication and hard work.

With a growth mindset, you're more likely to embrace challenges as opportunities for improvement. Sure, you might stumble and fall along the way, but that's all part of the journey. Remember, success isn't about avoiding failure; it's about learning from it and getting back up stronger than before!

Learning and Adaptation:
Life is a perpetual classroom, and challenges are its greatest teachers. Each challenge comes with a lesson, whether it's about ourselves, our skills, or the world around us. Embracing challenges means being open to learning and adapting our strategies accordingly.

Sometimes, the path we've chosen might not lead us to the desired outcome. But instead of getting discouraged, we can pivot and try a new approach. It's all about being flexible and understanding that growth often comes through trial and error.

Building Resilience:
Think of resilience as your superpower - the ability to bounce back from setbacks and keep going with newfound strength. Embracing challenges builds resilience like nothing else can. When you face difficult times head-on, you develop an inner fortitude that empowers you to face future obstacles with courage and determination.

Building resilience is not an overnight process; it's a journey of learning and growth. Each time you face a challenge and come out on the other side, you add another layer to your resilience, making you more capable of handling whatever life throws your way.

Stepping Out of Comfort Zones:
Ah, the comfort zone - that cozy, familiar space where everything feels safe and secure. But, guess what? The magic happens outside

of that comfort zone! Embracing challenges often requires taking a leap of faith and stepping into the unknown.

It's perfectly normal to feel a bit anxious when venturing into uncharted territory. But trust me, once you take that first step, you'll discover a whole new world of possibilities. Stepping out of your comfort zone allows you to grow, evolve, and tap into skills and strengths you never knew you had.

Overcoming Fear and Doubt:
Fear and doubt are like little gremlins that love to whisper in our ears and hold us back from embracing challenges. They tell us we're not good enough, that we're going to fail, and that it's better to play it safe. But here's the secret - EVERYONE feels fear and doubt at times!

The key is not to let these gremlins dictate your actions. Acknowledge your fears and doubts, but don't let them paralyze you. Take a deep breath, remind yourself of your capabilities, and face those challenges with a brave heart. You might be surprised at what you can achieve when you push past those little gremlins.

Celebrating Small Victories:
Life is a journey, and every journey is made up of steps - some big, some small. When you're embracing challenges, it's essential to celebrate those small victories along the way. Each little win, no matter how seemingly insignificant, contributes to your progress and keeps you motivated.

Don't wait for the big, flashy successes to pat yourself on the back. Celebrate the small wins - completing a difficult task, making progress on a project, or simply stepping out of your comfort zone. Acknowledging these achievements not only boosts your morale but also reminds you that you're on the right path, even when things get tough.

Conclusion:

Congratulations! You've just taken the first step on your journey to success - embracing challenges with open arms. By recognizing that challenges are opportunities for growth, learning, and self-discovery, you've unlocked a powerful tool that will help you navigate through life's twists and turns.

Remember, the growth mindset, learning, adaptation, resilience, stepping out of comfort zones, overcoming fear and doubt, and celebrating small victories are all part of the recipe for triumphing through adversity. So, keep that positive attitude, stay curious, and face those challenges with determination and a smile - you've got this!

Chapter 2
The Power of Resilience:
Bouncing Back Stronger

Life can be a rollercoaster ride with its share of ups and downs, but fear not! With resilience as your trusty sidekick, you'll learn to navigate the twists and turns with grace and emerge even stronger. So, fasten your seatbelt and let's explore how resilience can transform your life!

Understanding Resilience:
Resilience is like a superhero power we all possess - the ability to bounce back and recover from tough times. It's not about avoiding challenges; it's about facing them head-on and using them as stepping stones to grow and thrive. Picture resilience as a springboard that propels you forward, no matter how hard life's blows may be.

The beauty of resilience is that it's not fixed; it's a skill you can develop and strengthen over time. Every challenge you face provides an opportunity to flex that resilience muscle and grow even more resilient.

Embracing Adversity:

When life throws a curveball your way, it's natural to feel knocked off balance. But guess what? Resilience helps you find your footing again! Embracing adversity is the first step to building resilience. It's like acknowledging, "Hey, life is tough sometimes, but I'm tougher!"

Don't shy away from difficult situations or try to sweep them under the rug. Embrace them, face them, and know that you have the inner strength to endure and overcome. It's okay to feel overwhelmed, but remember, you're not alone on this journey.

Learning from Setbacks:
Resilience is not just about bouncing back; it's about learning and growing from setbacks. When life serves you lemons, make lemonade, right? Each setback is an opportunity for learning and self-improvement.

Take a moment to reflect on the experience and the lessons it brings. Ask yourself, "What can I learn from this situation?" The wisdom you gain from tough times will serve as a compass for navigating future challenges with greater insight and wisdom.

Cultivating Optimism:
Ah, optimism - the magical elixir of resilience!
Maintaining a positive outlook doesn't mean
you ignore life's difficulties; it means you approach them with hope and belief in yourself.
Optimism is like a ray of sunshine that pierces
through the darkest clouds.

Practice gratitude for the good things in your
life, and focus on the silver linings even during
tough times. Surround yourself with positive
influences, and be your own cheerleader. Remember, every cloud has a silver lining, and
optimism fuels your journey towards triumph.

Building a Support Network:
You know what they say: "No man is an is-
land." Resilience doesn't require you to go it a-
lone. In fact, having a strong support network
can make all the difference in the world.
Surround yourself with people who uplift, encourage, and inspire you.

Reach out to family, friends, mentors, or support groups when you face challenges. Sharing
your experiences and feelings with others not
only provides emotional support but also gives
you different perspectives and coping strategies.

Practicing Self-Compassion:
When the going gets tough, remember to be kind to yourself. Resilience isn't about being hard on yourself; it's about offering yourself the same compassion and understanding you'd give to a dear friend.

Acknowledge that it's okay to have moments of vulnerability and self-doubt. We all do! Treat yourself with gentleness and offer words of encouragement, just as you would to a friend going through a rough patch. Self-compassion nurtures resilience and helps you move forward with greater self-belief.

Embracing Change:
Life is a beautiful, ever-changing tapestry, and resilience is your best friend when it comes to adapting to change. Embrace change as a natural part of the journey - an opportunity for growth and transformation.

Resilience allows you to face uncertainty and unexpected turns with courage and flexibility. Remember that change can lead to new adventures, new opportunities, and even greater personal growth.

Conclusion:

You've now unlocked the incredible power of resilience, and it's yours to harness on this rollercoaster ride called life. Embracing adversity, learning from setbacks, cultivating optimism, building a support network, practicing self-compassion, and embracing change are the tools that will guide you through life's ups and downs.

Always remember that resilience is like a beacon of light that guides you through the darkest nights. You've got what it takes to bounce back stronger from any challenge that comes your way. Keep shining bright, my resilient friend, and let your indomitable spirit lead you to triumph and growth! Onward to a life filled with resilience and success!

Chapter 3
Conquering Self-Doubt: Building Unshakable Confidence

where we're going to tackle self-doubt head-on and build a Rock-solid foundation of unshakable confidence. Life is full of opportunities and adventures, but self-doubt can sometimes hold us back from fully embracing them. Don't be afraid! Together, we'll explore the secrets to conquering self-doubt and unlocking the true potential that lies within you. So, let's dive in and begin our journey to building unshakable confidence!

1. Embrace Your Uniqueness:

You, my friend, are one-of-a-kind, a true original! Embracing your uniqueness is the first step to conquering self-doubt. Recognize that your individuality is your superpower. The world is a colorful tapestry of diverse talents, skills, and perspectives, and you have a valuable contribution to make.

Instead of comparing yourself to others, celebrate your own strengths and qualities. Embrace your quirks and differences, for they are what make you extraordinary. Remember, there's no one quite like you, and that's a beautiful thing!

2. Challenge Negative Self-Talk:

Ah, that little voice in our heads that loves to sow seeds of self-doubt! It's time to stand up to that negative self-talk. Whenever you catch yourself thinking, "I can't do it" or "I'm not good enough," pause and challenge those thoughts.

Replace self-doubt with self-affirmation. Tell yourself, "I am capable," "I am deserving," and "I have what it takes." Over time, your positive self-talk will drown out the negativity, and you'll cultivate a mindset of confidence and self-belief.

3. Embrace the Power of "Yet":

Whenever you encounter a challenge or feel like you're not good at something, add a simple word to the end of the sentence: "yet." For example, "I can't do this... yet." This tiny word transforms your self-doubt into a growth mindset.

By acknowledging that you're a work in progress, you open yourself up to continuous learning and improvement. Remember, even the most accomplished individuals started from a place of "not yet," but with determination and practice, they became experts.

4. Celebrate Your Achievements:

You've achieved so much in life already, and it's time to celebrate those victories, big and small! Too often, we downplay our successes or dismiss them as mere luck. It's time to give yourself credit where credit is due.

Create a "success journal" where you jot down your achievements, no matter how minor they may seem. Celebrate each step forward, and acknowledge the hard work you put in. These moments of celebration will fuel your confidence and inspire you to achieve even greater things.

5. Step Out Of Your Comfort Zone:

Building confidence is like a muscle; it grows stronger with use. And one of the best ways to flex that confidence muscle is by stepping out of your comfort zone. Take on new challenges, try new experiences, and embrace the unknown.

Yes, it might feel scary at first, but that's where growth happens! Each time you step outside your comfort zone and succeed, you'll gain a surge of confidence that propels you to take on even bigger and bolder endeavors.

6. Seek Support and Encouragement:

Remember, you don't have to go it alone! Seek support and encouragement from your loved ones, mentors, or friends. Surround yourself with people who believe in you and lift you up.

When self-doubt creeps in, lean on your support network for a boost of confidence. They'll remind you of your strengths, encourage you to keep going, and provide a safety net for those moments when you stumble.

7. Learn from Setbacks:

Confidence doesn't mean you'll never face setbacks or make mistakes. It's about bouncing back stronger when you do encounter them. Embrace setbacks as opportunities for growth and learning.

Instead of beating yourself up over a mistake, ask yourself what you can learn from it. Every setback is a stepping stone towards improvement and future success. Embrace the idea that failure is not the end but a chance to begin again, wiser and more determined than before.

Conclusion:

You've now embarked on the path to conquering self-doubt and building unshakable confidence. Embrace your uniqueness, challenge negative self-talk, and remind yourself of the power of "yet." Celebrate your accomplishments, step out of your comfort zone, and seek support from your cheerleaders.

Confidence is not about being perfect; it's about believing in yourself and your abilities. It's the realization that you have what it takes to face life's challenges and achieve your dreams. You are more capable than you give yourself credit for, and the world is waiting for you to shine your light brightly!

So, go forth with confidence, my amazing friend, and embrace the journey of self-belief and personal growth. You've got this, and I'm cheering you on every step of the way! Onward to a life filled with unshakable confidence and boundless possibilities!

Chapter 4
Turning Setbacks into Opportunities: Finding Silver Linings

where we'll embark on a journey to discover the magic of turning setbacks into opportunities and finding silver linings in every cloud. Life has a funny way of throwing curveballs our way, but fear not! With the right mindset and a dash of positivity, you'll learn how to transform challenges into stepping stones to success. So, let's dive into the art of finding silver linings and embracing setbacks as opportunities for growth!

1. Embrace the Power of Perspective:

When faced with setbacks, it's easy to feel disappointed or defeated. But let me share a secret with you - the power lies in how we perceive these challenges. Instead of viewing setbacks as roadblocks, see them as detours on your journey. These detours might lead you to exciting new paths you never imagined!

Shift your perspective from "Why is this happening to me?" to "What can I learn from this experience?" Embrace setbacks as opportunities to grow, learn, and become stronger. Remember, it's not what happens to you that defines you, but how you respond to it.

2. Seek the Silver Linings:

In every cloud, there's a silver lining waiting to be discovered. When facing setbacks, train yourself to seek out those silver linings. Even in the most challenging situations, there's always something positive to be found.

Ask yourself, "What can I gain from this experience?" or "What doors might open because of this setback?" Finding the silver linings helps you shift your focus from the negative to the positive, and that shift in focus can make all the difference.

3. Embrace the Gift of Growth:

Setbacks are not failures; they are opportunities for growth. Every challenge you face provides an opportunity to learn, improve, and become a better version of yourself. Embrace setbacks as stepping stones on your path to greatness.

Think of life as a classroom, and setbacks as the lessons that propel you forward. Each setback teaches you something valuable, whether it's about your strengths, weaknesses, or resilience. Embrace the gift of growth that setbacks offer you.

4. Cultivate Resilience and Adaptability:

Setbacks can be tough, but they also make you more resilient and adaptable. Embracing setbacks means learning to bounce back stronger, even when life throws you off balance.

Cultivate resilience by acknowledging your emotions and seeking support when needed. Adaptability allows you to adjust your approach and find new solutions when faced with challenges. Together, resilience and adaptability empower you to face any setback with grace and determination.

5. See Setbacks as Opportunities for Innovation:

Some of the greatest innovations and breakthroughs in history emerged from setbacks and failures. Embrace setbacks as opportunities to think outside the box, explore new possibilities, and innovate.

When facing a setback, ask yourself, "How can I approach this differently?" or "What creative solutions can I explore?" Every setback is an opportunity to redefine your approach and potentially discover a more effective path forward.

6. Celebrate Progress, Not Perfection:

In a world obsessed with perfection, it's easy to be discouraged by setbacks. But let me tell you a little secret - progress is more important than perfection. Embrace setbacks as part of the journey to success, and celebrate the progress you make along the way.

Each setback you encounter brings you one step closer to your goals. Celebrate the effort you put in, the lessons you learn, and the steps you take towards your dreams. Remember, success is not a straight line; it's a winding path with ups and downs.

7. Practice Gratitude:

Gratitude is like a superpower that can transform how we perceive setbacks. When you cultivate a grateful heart, you shift your focus from what's lacking to what you already have.

Even in the face of setbacks, find things to be grateful for - your support network, the lessons you've learned, or the strength you've discovered within yourself. Gratitude not only helps you find silver linings but also brings a sense of peace and contentment amidst challenges.

Conclusion:

You've now mastered the art of turning setbacks into opportunities and finding silver linings in every cloud. Embrace setbacks with a positive perspective, seek the silver linings, and embrace the gift of growth that they offer.

Cultivate resilience and adaptability, seeing setbacks as opportunities for innovation and progress. Celebrate your progress, practice gratitude, and remember that setbacks are simply detours on your journey to success.

With the power of finding silver linings, setbacks become not stumbling blocks, but stepping stones to a brighter and more fulfilling future. Embrace the journey, and know that with the right mindset, you can conquer any challenge that comes your way. Onward to a life filled with opportunities and silver lining

Chapter 5
Cultivating a Growth Mindset: Embracing Change and Learning

where we're going to explore the wonders of cultivating a growth mindset. Life is a never-ending journey of learning and growth, and with a growth mindset, you'll navigate this journey with enthusiasm and a thirst for knowledge. So, buckle up, and let's dive into the world of embracing change and continuous learning!

1. Understanding the Growth Mindset:

At the heart of a growth mindset is the belief that our abilities and intelligence can be developed through dedication and effort. It's like having a secret superpower that allows you to embrace challenges as opportunities for growth and learning.

With a growth mindset, you'll stop seeing failures as the end of the road and start viewing them as stepping stones to success. Embrace the power of "not yet" - recognizing that you may not have mastered something YET, but y-ou're on the path to improvement.

2. Embrace Change as a Constant:

Change is the only constant in life, and a growth mindset welcomes it with open arms. Instead of fearing change, see it as an opportunity for personal and professional development.

When faced with change, remind yourself that it brings new possibilities and experiences. Embrace the unknown and step into it with curiosity and an open mind. Change is not a threat; it's an adventure waiting to unfold.

3. Embrace Challenges with Enthusiasm:

A growth mindset is like a cheerleader that motivates you to take on challenges with enthusiasm. Challenges are not roadblocks; they are stepping stones to new heights.

Embrace challenges with the belief that you can learn and improve from every experience.

Don't shy away from difficult tasks; instead, approach them with determination and a positive attitude.

4. Emphasize Effort and Learning:

In a growth mindset, the focus is on effort and learning rather than innate talent. Instead of thinking, "I'm just not good at this," shift your mindset to, "I can improve with practice and learning."

Celebrate the effort you put into your endeavors, regardless of the outcome. Recognize that every step forward, no matter how small, is progress. The journey of learning is as important as the destination.

5. Embrace Setbacks as Learning Opportunities:

Setbacks are not signs of failure; they are valuable learning opportunities. With a growth mindset, you'll see setbacks as an opportunity to reflect, learn, and adapt.

Ask yourself, "What can I learn from this set-back?" or "How can I approach this differently next time?" Each setback brings you one step closer to mastery. Embrace the process of learning from every experience.

6. Seek Feedback and Constructive Criticism:

In a growth mindset, feedback and constructive criticism are gifts, not threats. Embrace the input from others as an opportunity to learn and grow.

Be open to feedback, both positive and constructive, and use it to improve yourself. See it as an opportunity to gain new perspectives and insights that can propel you forward.

7. Encourage a Culture of Growth:

If you're part of a team or community, encourage a culture of growth mindset. Celebrate effort, learning, and progress in others and yourself.

Supporting and uplifting each other, embracing challenges together and inspiring one another to reach new heights. When everyone cultivates a growth mindset, the collective potential for growth and success is boundless.

Conclusion:

You've unlocked the wonders of cultivating a growth mindset, embracing change, and continuous learning. Embrace challenges, see setbacks as opportunities, and emphasize effort and learning in your journey.

Embrace change with enthusiasm and view feedback as valuable gifts. Encourage a culture of growth and learning in yourself and those around you. With a growth mindset, you'll navigate life's challenges with grace and curiosity, knowing that every experience is an opportunity for growth.

Remember, the journey of learning and improvement is a lifelong adventure, and with a growth mindset, you'll continue to flourish and thrive. Embrace change, embrace learning, and embrace the power of growth. Onward to a life filled with continuous growth and endless possibilities! You've got this!

Chapter 6
Overcoming Fear:
Stepping Out of Comfort Zones

where we're going to dive deep into the realm of overcoming fear and embracing the magic that happens when we step out of our comfort zones. Fear can hold us back from living our fullest lives, but fear not (pun intended)! With the right mindset and a dash of courage, you'll learn how to conquer those fears and unleash your true potential. So, let's embark on this thrilling journey of stepping out of comfort zones!

1. Acknowledge Your Fears:

The first step to overcoming fear is to acknowledge it. It's perfectly normal to feel fear when facing the unknown or trying something new. Instead of suppressing those feelings, embrace them as a natural part of the process.

Recognize that fear is not a sign of weakness but a sign of growth. Every great adventure begins with a little apprehension, so give yourself a pat on the back for being brave enough to acknowledge your fears.

2. Define Your Comfort Zone:

Your comfort zone is that cozy space where you feel safe and familiar. It's where you know the ropes and feel at ease. While comfort zones are nice, staying in them for too long can limit your potential for growth.

Identify the boundaries of your comfort zone. What activities or situations make you feel comfortable, and which ones make you feel anxious? Knowing your comfort zone will help you understand where you need to push yourself to grow.

3. Set Small Goals:

Stepping out of your comfort zone doesn't mean you have to take a giant leap into the unknown. Start by setting small, achievable goals that slightly stretch your boundaries.

If public speaking makes you nervous, for example, challenge yourself to share an idea in a small group setting first. As you accomplish these mini-goals, you'll gain confidence and momentum to take on more significant challenges.

4. Prepare and Educate Yourself:

Knowledge is power, and when you're stepping out of your comfort zone, preparation can be your best friend. Educate yourself about the situation or activity you're facing.

Whether it's starting a new job, traveling to an unfamiliar place, or trying a new hobby, gather information and equip yourself with the tools you need to navigate the experience confidently.

5. Embrace a Growth Mindset:

Remember our old friend, the growth mindset? Embrace it wholeheartedly when confronting your fears. View challenges as opportunities for learning and personal development.

Rather than fear failure, see it as a stepping stone to success. With a growth mindset, you'll view stepping out of your comfort zone not as a threat but as an exciting adventure filled with possibilities.

6. Visualize Success:

Visualization is a powerful technique used by athletes, performers, and successful individuals to overcome fear and achieve greatness. Take a moment to close your eyes and visualize yourself succeeding in the situation that causes you fear.

Imagine every detail vividly - how you feel, what you see, and the sense of accomplishment. Visualization can rewire your brain to associate positivity with the experience, making it easier to step out of your comfort zone with confidence.

7. Celebrate Your Efforts:

Remember to celebrate every step you take outside of your comfort zone, no matter the outcome. Acknowledge your bravery and the effort you put into facing your fears.

Even if things don't go as planned, pat yourself on the back for having the courage to try. Celebrate the growth and the learning experience, as each step takes you closer to living a more fulfilling and adventurous life.

Conclusion:

You've now discovered the art of overcoming fear and stepping out of your comfort zones. Acknowledge your fears, define your comfort zone, and set small, achievable goals to push your boundaries.

Prepare yourself with knowledge and embrace a growth mindset. Visualize success, and most importantly, celebrate every effort you make to face your fears.

With each step you take outside of your comfort zone, you'll grow stronger, more confident, and ready to embrace life's exciting opportunities. Remember, the magic happens when you dare to step into the unknown. So, let your courage guide you, and don't be afraid, for you are capable of extraordinary things! Onward to a life filled with thrilling adventures and endless possibilities! You've got this!

Chapter 7
Harnessing Inner Strength:
Navigating Life's Storms

where we'll delve into the art of harnessing inner strength to navigate the storms that life may throw our way. Life is a beautiful journey, but it's not always smooth sailing. Fear not! Within you lies a wellspring of strength, courage, and resilience that will guide you through the toughest of times. So, let's embark on this empowering journey of harnessing your inner strength and weathering life's storms with grace and determination.

1. Embrace Your Resilient Spirit:

Before we dive in, take a moment to acknowledge the resilient spirit within you. Think about the challenges you've overcome, the setbacks you've bounced back from, and the tough times you've endured. Recognize that you are stronger and more capable than you may realize.

Embrace the truth that you've survived every storm that life has brought your way, and that resilience resides deep within your heart. You've got this, and you'll conquer whatever comes your way!

2. Accept the Ebb and Flow of Life:

Just like the tides of the ocean, life has its ebb and flow. Storms will come, and storms will go. Embrace the natural rhythm of life and understand that both sunshine and rain are part of the journey.

When facing a storm, accept that it's a temporary part of your journey. Trust that after the rain, the sun will shine again. With this acceptance, you'll find the strength to navigate through the darkest times.

3. Lean on Your Support Network:

In the face of a storm, you don't have to brave it alone. Your support network is there to lift

you up, provide a listening ear, and offer a helping hand.

Reach out to your loved ones, friends, or
mentors when you need support. Their
presence and encouragement will remind you
that you're not alone on this journey, and together, you'll weather the storm.

4. Practice Self-Compassion:

In the midst of life's storms, it's essential to
be gentle with yourself. Practice self-compassion and treat yourself with kindness and understanding.

Acknowledge that it's okay to feel overwhelmed or vulnerable. Offer yourself the same
compassion you would give to a dear friend
going through a rough patch. Remember, you
are doing the best you can, and that's enough.

5. Focus on What You Can Control:

During storms, it's natural to feel a lack of control. Instead of dwelling on what you can't control, shift your focus to what you can.

Identify the actions you can take to navigate through the storm, and focus on those. Whether it's making small steps forward or seeking professional help, taking control of what you can empowers you to face the challenges with greater clarity and strength.

6. Find Solace in Mindfulness:

Mindfulness is a powerful tool to find peace amidst life's storms. Take time to practice mindfulness, be present in the moment, and observe your thoughts and feelings without judgment.

When faced with uncertainty or adversity, mindfulness can ground you and help you regain focus. It's a way of calming the storm within, allowing you to approach challenges with a clear and centered mind.

7. Seek the Lessons in the Storms:

Every storm brings with it valuable lessons. As you navigate through life's challenges, seek the wisdom and insights that these experiences offer.

Ask yourself, "What can I learn from this storm?" or "How can I grow from this experience?" Embrace the storms as opportunities for personal growth and discovery. When the clouds clear, you'll emerge wiser and more resilient than before.

Conclusion:

You've harnessed your inner strength and discovered the art of navigating life's storms with grace and determination. Embrace your resilient spirit, accept the ebb and flow of life, and lean on your support network.

Practice self-compassion, focus on what you can control, and find solace in mindfulness. Seek the lessons in the storms, knowing that they are opportunities for growth and empowerment.

Remember, you are a force to be reckoned with, capable of weathering any storm that comes your way. Embrace life's challenges with courage and determination, for within you lies the strength to conquer whatever lies ahead.

Onward to a life filled with resilience, growth, and an unyielding spirit! You've got this, and the storms of life will never overpower your inner light! Keep shining brightly, my courageous friend!

Chapter 8
Building a Supportive Network: The Role of Relationships in Success

where we'll explore the incredible role of relationships in your journey to success. Life is a beautiful tapestry woven with the threads of connections, and building a supportive network of relationships can be a powerful catalyst for achieving your dreams. So, let's spread our wings and dive into the world of nurturing meaningful connections and the immense impact they have on your path to success.

1. The Power of Relationships:

Humans are social beings, and our connections with others play a pivotal role in our lives. Relationships are like seeds of possibility; they can nurture our growth and propel us towards our goals.

Understand that building meaningful relationships isn't just about networking for personal gain; it's about creating a support system that uplifts and inspires you. The power of relationships lies in the genuine connections we forge with others.

2. Identify Your Circle:

Take a moment to identify the people in your life who truly support and believe in you. These can be family members, friends, mentors, colleagues, or like-minded individuals.

Recognize the positive impact each person has had on your journey and cherish these relationships. Your circle is your tribe, and together, you can achieve remarkable things.

3. Nurture Reciprocity:

Building a supportive network is a two-way street. Just as you seek support, be willing to offer your support to others as well.

Nurture reciprocity in your relationships by being a good listener, providing encouragement, and celebrating the successes of those around you. Remember, a rising tide lifts all boats, and supporting others can elevate your own journey to success.

4. Seek Diverse Perspectives:

Surround yourself with a diverse network of individuals from different backgrounds, professions, and perspectives. Diversity enriches your experiences and broadens your horizons.

Engaging with people who think differently challenges your assumptions and allows for creative problem-solving. Embrace the beauty of diversity in your network.

5. Embrace Authenticity:

In your relationships, be authentic and genuine. Be true to yourself and let your unique personality shine.

Authenticity creates deep and meaningful connections, as people are drawn to your genuine self. Remember, you don't need to wear a mask to be accepted; your authenticity is your superpower.

6. Communicate with Empathy:

Communication is the lifeblood of relationships. Practice empathy and active listening when interacting with others.

Seek to understand their perspectives and feelings, and respond with compassion. Empathy fosters trust and creates an environment where support and understanding thrive.

7. Celebrate Each Other's Successes:

In a supportive network, celebrating each other's successes is a key ingredient. When someone in your circle achieves a milestone, cheer them on with genuine joy.

Sharing in each other's successes strengthens the bond between you and encourages a culture of support and encouragement.

Conclusion:

You've now discovered the vital role of relationships in your journey to success. Build a supportive network of meaningful connections, nurture reciprocity, and embrace diversity and authenticity.

Practice empathetic communication and celebrate each other's successes. Your supportive network is like a tapestry of inspiration, weaving together the threads of encouragement, guidance, and belief into one another.

As you continue to foster these relationships, know that you are never alone on your journey to success. Your supportive network will be there to uplift, inspire, and celebrate with you every step of the way.

So, spread your wings and soar high with the power of your connections. Together, you and your supportive network will create a symphony of success, achieving dreams beyond imagination. Onward to a life filled with meaningful connections and boundless achievements! You've got this, and your network has your back!

Chapter 9
The Art of Adaptability:
Thriving in a Dynamic World

where we'll dive into the art of adaptability and discover how to thrive in a dynamic and ever-changing world. Life is like a dance, with twists and turns that can lead us to unexpected places. Embracing the power of adaptability allows us to flow gracefully with these changes and make the most out of every situation. So, let's put on our dancing shoes and explore the wonders of adaptability in this friendly and insightful journey.

1. Understanding the Nature of Change:

Change is a constant companion in life. It's like the seasons, shifting from spring to summer, and from autumn to winter. Embrace the understanding that change is a natural part of the journey.

Adaptability is not about resisting change, but about embracing it with an open mind and a positive attitude. When you accept change as a friend rather than a foe, you'll find the power to navigate through life's twists and turns with grace.

2. Cultivate a Growth Mindset:

Ah, our old friend, the growth mindset! Cultivating this mindset is the foundation of adaptability. Embrace the belief that you can learn, grow, and adapt to new situations.

View challenges as opportunities for learning and see setbacks as stepping stones to success. With a growth mindset, you'll be ready to embrace change and turn it into a powerful force for personal and professional development.

3. Embrace Flexibility:

Adaptability is like being a bamboo tree - flexible and resilient. When the winds of change blow, the bamboo bends gracefully but does not break.

Embrace flexibility in your thoughts and actions. Be open to new ideas, different perspectives, and alternative approaches. The more flexible you are, the better you can adapt to any situation that comes your way.

4. Embrace Lifelong Learning:

In a dynamic world, learning is a lifelong adventure. Stay curious and embrace learning opportunities with enthusiasm.

Seek new knowledge, develop new skills, and be open to continuous growth. Lifelong learning equips you with the tools you need to adapt and thrive in an ever-changing world.

5. Stay Calm in Uncertainty:

When faced with uncertainty, it's natural to feel anxious or overwhelmed. But remember, uncertainty also brings new possibilities.

Practice mindfulness and staying present in the moment. When you stay calm amidst uncertainty, you create space for creativity and resourcefulness to emerge.

6. Focus on Solutions:

Adaptability is about finding solutions rather than dwelling on problems. When challenges arise, shift your focus to what you can do to overcome them.

Seek solutions with a positive and proactive mindset. Embrace the power of "yet" - acknowledging that you may not have the answer now, but you can find it with effort and persistence.

7. Embrace Change as an Opportunity:

Embrace the idea that change is not something to be feared, but an opportunity for growth and new experiences.

When faced with change, ask yourself, "What can I gain from this experience?" or "How can I use this as an opportunity to improve?" Embracing change as an opportunity will empower you to adapt and thrive in the face of uncertainty.

Conclusion:

You've now mastered the art of adaptability and learned how to thrive in a dynamic world. Understand the nature of change, cultivate a growth mindset, and embrace flexibility.

Embrace lifelong learning and stay calm in uncertainty. Focus on solutions and see change as an opportunity for growth.

As you continue to dance with the twists and turns of life, remember that adaptability is your superpower. With the ability to adapt, you can navigate any situation with grace and resilience.

So, put on your dancing shoes and step into the dynamic world with confidence. Embrace change, and know that you have the power to thrive no matter what comes your way. Onward to a life filled with adaptability and endless possibilities! You've got this, and the dance of life is waiting for your graceful moves!

Chapter 10
Persistence Pays Off:
Staying the Course on the Journey

where we'll explore the incredible power of persistence and how it can lead you to the destination of your dreams. Life's journey is filled with twists and turns, ups and downs, but fear not! With unwavering persistence and a friendly attitude, you'll conquer any challenges that come your way. So, let's embark on this tenacious journey and discover how staying the course can lead you to extraordinary success.

1. Embrace the Power of Persistence:

Persistence is like a compass that guides you through the darkest of times. It's the ability to keep moving forward, even when faced with obstacles and setbacks.

Understand that success rarely comes overnight. Embrace the journey with the understanding that it may require time, effort, and determination. With persistence, you'll have the strength to weather any storm and come out stronger on the other side.

2. Set Clear Goals:

To stay the course on your journey, set clear and achievable goals. These goals act as signposts, keeping you focused and motivated.

Break your big dreams into smaller, manageable milestones. Celebrate each achievement along the way, as each step forward brings you closer to the destination.

3. Cultivate a Positive Mindset:

A positive mindset is like sunshine on a cloudy day. It fuels your persistence and keeps your spirits high.

When faced with challenges, adopt an optimistic outlook. See setbacks as temporary roadblocks and not permanent dead-ends. A positive mindset enables you to stay motivated and resilient in the face of adversity.

4. Learn from Setbacks:

Setbacks are not failures; they are opportunities to learn and grow. Embrace them with curiosity and seek the lessons they offer.

When you encounter setbacks, ask yourself, "What can I learn from this experience?" or "How can I improve for the next time?" With each setback, you gain valuable insights that can refine your approach and lead to eventual success.

5. Seek Support and Encouragement:

On your journey, you don't have to walk alone. Seek support and encouragement from your support network.

Lean on your friends, family, mentors, or like-minded individuals. Their support can provide you with the motivation and strength to persevere when the going gets tough.

6. Stay Flexible Yet Persistent:

While persistence is vital, flexibility is equally important. Stay open to adapting your strategies and approaches as needed.

The path to success may not always be linear. Be willing to adjust your course, but never lose sight of your ultimate goal. Stay persistent in your pursuit while remaining flexible in your methods.

7. Celebrate Your Progress:

As you stay the course on your journey, celebrate your progress along the way. Acknowledge your effort and the steps you've taken.

Celebrate not only the big wins but also the small victories that contribute to your growth. By recognizing your progress, you'll fuel your motivation to keep pushing forward.

Conclusion:

You've now discovered the incredible power of persistence and learned how to stay the course on your journey to success. Embrace persistence as your faithful companion, guiding you through challenges and setbacks.

Set clear goals and cultivate a positive mindset that keeps you focused and resilient. Learn from setbacks, seek support, and stay flexible while remaining steadfast in your pursuit.

Celebrate your progress and remember that every step forward, no matter how small, brings you closer to your dreams.

So, stay the course with unwavering determination and a friendly spirit. With persistence as your guide, you can conquer any challenges that come your way and achieve extraordinary success. Onward to a life filled with tenacity and triumph! You've got this, and the journey ahead is waiting for your unstoppable stride!

Chapter 11
Embracing Failure: Learning from Mistakes and Moving Forward

where we'll explore the transformative power of embracing failure and turning it into a stepping stone for growth. Failure is not a dead end; it's a detour that leads us to valuable lessons and new opportunities. So, don't be afraid of the stumbles and fumbles on your journey. With a friendly attitude and a growth mindset, you'll learn to embrace failure, extract its wisdom, and move forward stronger than ever before.

1. Rethinking Failure:

Let's start by redefining failure. It's not a reflection of your worth or abilities. Instead, it's a natural part of the learning process.

Embrace the belief that failure is an opportunity for growth and improvement. When you see it in this light, you'll no longer fear it but welcome it as a necessary part of your journey.

2. Extracting Lessons:

When faced with failure, take a moment to reflect on the experience. What can you learn from it? What went wrong, and what could be done differently next time?

Failures often provide valuable insights into our strengths, weaknesses, and blind spots. Embrace them as your most potent teachers, offering you the wisdom you need to evolve and succeed.

3. Cultivate a Growth Mindset:

Ah, our trusty companion, the growth mindset! Cultivating this mindset is essential when embracing failure.

With a growth mindset, you'll view failure not as a roadblock but as a stepping stone to success. It's a belief that your abilities can be developed through effort and learning. This perspective empowers you to keep pushing forward, even in the face of failure.

4. Banish Self-Judgment:

When failure knocks on your door, avoid falling into the trap of self-judgment and self-criticism. Remember, you're only human, and making mistakes is part of the human experience.

Be kind to yourself and offer self-compassion. Treat yourself as you would a dear friend who's going through a rough time. By doing so, you'll build resilience and strength to bounce back from failure.

5. Reframe Failure as Feedback:

Instead of seeing failure as a personal defeat, reframe it as feedback on your journey. It's an indication of what didn't work and what adjustments are needed.

Use failure as a guide to refine your strategies and approaches. Each failure brings you closer to finding the winning formula.

6. Take Risks and Embrace Vulnerability:

Failure often accompanies risk-taking and vulnerability. But remember, taking risks is essential to growth and success.

Embrace the courage to step outside your comfort zone and take calculated risks. Even if it doesn't work out as planned, you'll gain experience and wisdom that will serve you well in the future.

7. Celebrate Progress, Not Perfection:

In a world fixated on perfection, it's easy to be discouraged by failure. But let me tell you a secret - progress is more important than perfection.

Celebrate every effort you put in and every step you take towards your goals. Remember, failure is not the end; it's a stepping stone on the path to success.

Conclusion:

You've now discovered the transformative power of embracing failure and turning it into a force for growth. Rethink failure, extract its valuable lessons, and cultivate a growth mindset that propels you forward.

Banish self-judgment and reframe failure as feedback. Take risks, embrace vulnerability, and celebrate progress over perfection.

With this newfound perspective on failure, you'll fearlessly embrace challenges, knowing that even in the face of setbacks, you're on the path to greatness.

So, move forward with a friendly spirit, embracing failure as a friend and teacher on your journey to success. Embrace the stumbles, for they will lead you to soar to heights beyond your imagination. Onward to a life filled with wisdom, resilience, and the courage to embrace failure with open arms! You've got this, and your journey is destined for greatness!

Chapter 12
The Resilience of the Human Spirit:
Triumphing over Tragedy

where we'll explore the awe-inspiring resilience of the human spirit and how it triumphs over tragedy. Life's journey is not always smooth, and tragedy may strike unexpectedly, but fear not! Within you lies an indomitable spirit that can overcome even the darkest of times. So, let's embark on this powerful journey of resilience and discover how the human spirit shines brightest in the face of adversity, all in a friendly and compassionate tone.

1. Understanding Resilience:

Resilience is like a flame that flickers but never goes out. It's the ability to bounce back and thrive in the face of adversity.

Life can throw unexpected challenges our way - loss, illness, or upheaval - but resilience allows us to stand tall despite the storm. Understand that resilience is not about avoiding pain or tragedy but about navigating through it with strength and courage. It's a testament to the human spirit's capacity to rise above even the most challenging circumstances.

2. Acknowledging the Impact of Tragedy:

When tragedy strikes, it can feel like the ground beneath us has crumbled. It's essential to acknowledge the impact of tragedy and allow yourself to grieve and process the emotions.

Know that it's okay to feel a range of emotions - sadness, anger, fear, or confusion. Embrace the support of loved ones during this time, for they can provide comfort and solace. Remember, you don't have to go through this alone.

3. Finding Meaning in Adversity:

As you begin to heal, seek meaning in the midst of adversity. While tragedy may be painful, it may also lead to growth and transformation.

Ask yourself, "What can I learn from this experience?" or "How can I use this as an opportunity for personal growth?" Finding meaning in tragedy can empower you to turn pain into purpose.

Perhaps your experience can inspire and help others facing similar challenges. Embracing a sense of purpose can add meaning to your journey and be a source of strength during difficult times.

4. Cultivating Inner Strength:

The human spirit is like a diamond, forged under pressure, and made stronger with each trial. Cultivate your inner strength as you navigate through adversity.

Practice self-care, mindfulness, and gratitude. These practices can nourish your spirit and provide you with the strength to face the darkest times. Allow yourself moments of quiet reflection, where you can connect with your inner self and find solace in the present moment.

5. Embracing Support:

You don't have to carry the weight of tragedy alone. Embrace the support of your friends, family, or a professional counselor.

Sharing your emotions and experiences with others can provide relief and healing. The connections with your support network can be a lifeline during challenging times. Openly express your feelings and allow others to be there for you.

6. Taking One Step at a Time:

Remember that healing is a process, and it's okay to take it one step at a time. Be patient with yourself as you move forward.

Set small, achievable goals and celebrate every progress, no matter how small. Each step forward is a testament to your resilience and strength. Allow yourself to rest and recharge, knowing that taking care of yourself is an essential part of the healing journey.

7. Celebrating the Triumph:

As you move through tragedy and emerge on the other side, celebrate your triumphs - both big and small.

Celebrate the moments when you found the strength to keep going, the times when you reached out for support, and the courage you showed in facing the darkness.

Remember that triumph doesn't mean erasing the pain, but rather learning to carry it with grace and resilience. Your triumph lies in your ability to endure, grow, and find hope even in the face of adversity.

Conclusion:

You've now discovered the remarkable resilience of the human spirit and how it triumphs over tragedy. Embrace the power of resilience, acknowledging its ability to help you rise above life's darkest challenges.

Allow yourself to grieve and find meaning in adversity. Cultivate inner strength through self-care, mindfulness, and gratitude.

Embrace the support of your loved ones, and remember, you are never alone on this journey. Take it one step at a time, celebrating every triumph along the way.

With resilience as your ally, you can triumph over tragedy and emerge stronger, wiser, and more compassionate. Onward to a life filled with the light of resilience and the courage to embrace life's challenges with an unyielding spirit! You've got this, and the triumph of your spirit shines brightly for the world to see!

Chapter 13
Discovering Purpose:
The Fuel for Triumph

where we'll delve into the profound journey of discovering your purpose and how it fuels your triumphs in life. Life becomes truly meaningful when we find our purpose, the North Star that guides our actions and ignites our passions. So, let's embark on this soul-stirring exploration of purpose, all in a friendly and encouraging tone.

1. The Quest for Purpose:

The search for purpose is like an adventure, filled with twists and turns that lead us to self-discovery. Understand that purpose is not a destination but a journey of exploration and self-awareness.

Ask yourself questions like, "What brings me joy?" or "What impact do I want to make in the world?" Embrace the quest for purpose with curiosity and an open heart.

2. Aligning with Your Passions:

Purpose and passion are intertwined like two dancers in perfect harmony. Discovering your purpose often involves aligning with your deepest passions and values.

Reflect on what activities light up your soul and fill you with enthusiasm. It's in these moments that you may find glimpses of your purpose calling out to you.

3. Embracing Your Unique Gifts:

Each of us possesses unique gifts and talents, waiting to be uncovered. Embrace your strengths and acknowledge the unique contribution you can make to the world.

Recognize that your gifts are not just for personal gain but can be utilized to serve others and contribute to the greater good. Embracing your gifts empowers you to live a purpose-driven life.

4. Seeking Impact and Meaning:

Purpose often emerges from the desire to make a positive impact on the world around us. Consider how you can use your talents and passions to create meaningful change.

Ask yourself, "How can I use my strengths to help others?" or "What legacy do I want to leave behind?" Seeking impact and meaning in your actions infuses your life with purpose.

5. Connecting with Your Values:

Your values are the compass that points you towards your purpose. Reflect on what matters most to you in life - honesty, compassion, growth, or creativity.

As you connect with your values, you'll find that they align with your purpose and guide you toward decisions and actions that bring you closer to triumph.

6. Embracing the Journey:

Discovering purpose is not a linear process but a beautiful journey of self-discovery. Embrace the moments of uncertainty and be patient with yourself.

Allow your purpose to unfold naturally, trusting that you are on the right path. Each step you take towards understanding your purpose is a triumph in itself.

7. Living Your Purpose:

Once you've discovered your purpose, let it be the driving force behind your actions. Live your purpose every day, and let it be the fuel for your triumphs.

Infuse purpose into your personal and professional life. Use it as a source of motivation when faced with challenges or setbacks. Your purpose will empower you to overcome obstacles and achieve remarkable triumphs.

Conclusion:

You've now embarked on the soul-stirring journey of discovering your purpose and understanding its role as the fuel for triumph in your life.

Continue the quest for purpose with curiosity and an open heart. Align with your passions and embrace your unique gifts. Seek impact and meaning in your actions, and connect with your values as your compass.

Embrace the beauty of the journey and be patient with yourself as you discover your purpose. Once discovered, let your purpose be the driving force behind your actions, empowering you to triumph in every aspect of your life.

Onward to a life filled with purpose and triumph! You've got this, and your purpose is like a guiding star that will lead you to incredible heights of fulfillment and achievement!

Chapter 14
Overcoming Obstacles:
The Roadblocks to Success

where we'll delve into the art of overcoming obstacles on your journey to success. Life's path is not always smooth, and obstacles may appear like roadblocks in your way. But fear not! With a friendly attitude and a determined spirit, you'll learn how to navigate through these challenges and emerge stronger on the other side. So, let's embark on this empowering journey of overcoming obstacles with grace and tenacity.

1. Understanding Obstacles:

Obstacles are like puzzles waiting to be solved. They are the tests that challenge your determination and resilience.

Recognize that obstacles are a natural part of any worthwhile pursuit. Instead of seeing them as barriers, see them as opportunities for growth and learning.

2. Embracing a Positive Mindset:

A positive mindset is like a shield that protects you from negativity and doubt. Embrace the belief that you can overcome any obstacle that comes your way.

When faced with challenges, focus on solutions rather than dwelling on the problem. A positive mindset empowers you to approach obstacles with determination and creativity.

3. Breaking Down the Obstacles:

Big obstacles can feel overwhelming, but remember, they can often be broken down into smaller, manageable tasks.

Identify the specific challenges within the obstacle and create a plan of action to address them one step at a time. Breaking down the obstacles makes them more approachable and achievable.

4. Seeking support:

You don't have to face obstacles alone. Seek support from your friends, family, or mentors.

Reach out to your support network when you need advice or encouragement. Sharing your challenges with others can offer new perspectives and solutions.

5. Learning from Setbacks:

Obstacles may sometimes lead to setbacks, but setbacks are not failures. Embrace them as opportunities for learning and growth.

Reflect on what went wrong, what lessons can be learned, and how you can improve for the future. Each setback is a chance to refine your approach and move closer to success.

6. Building resilience:

Resilience is your greatest ally in overcoming obstacles. Cultivate your resilience by practicing self-care, mindfulness, and positive coping mechanisms.

When facing challenges, remind yourself of the times you've overcome adversity in the past. Draw strength from those experiences to face the current obstacles with courage.

7. Celebrating Progress:

As you work to overcome obstacles, celebrate every progress, no matter how small.

Each step forward, each effort made, is a triumph in itself. Acknowledge your achievements, and be kind to yourself during this process.

Conclusion:

You've now discovered the art of overcoming obstacles on your journey to success. Understand that obstacles are opportunities for growth, not roadblocks to your dreams.

Embrace a positive mindset, break down the challenges, and seek support from your loved ones. Learn from setbacks and build your resilience as you face the obstacles head-on.

Celebrate every progress and remember that overcoming obstacles is a testament to your determination and strength.

Onward to a life filled with grace, tenacity, and the ability to conquer any obstacles that come your way! You've got this, and the road to success is paved with your unwavering spirit!

Chapter 15
The Transformative Power of Gratitude: Focusing on the Positives

where we'll explore the incredible transformative power of gratitude and how it allows you to focus on the positives in life. Gratitude is like a magical lens that shifts your perspective, helping you see the beauty and blessings even in the midst of challenges. So, let's embark on this heartwarming journey of gratitude, all in a friendly and uplifting tone.

1. Understanding Gratitude:

Gratitude is like sunshine for the soul. It's the practice of acknowledging and appreciating the good things in life, both big and small.

Understand that gratitude is not just a fleeting feeling but a way of life. It's a conscious choice to focus on the positives and be mindful of the blessings surrounding you.

2. Counting Your Blessings:

At the heart of gratitude lies the act of counting your blessings. Take a moment each day to reflect on the things you are grateful for.

It could be the love of your family, the support of your friends, or even the simple pleasures like a warm cup of tea or a beautiful sunset. Cultivate the habit of gratitude by recognizing the abundance in your life.

3. Shifting Perspective:

Gratitude is like a pair of glasses that helps you see the silver linings in every situation. When faced with challenges, shift your perspective to find the lessons and opportunities they bring.

Ask yourself, "What can I learn from this experience?" or "How can I grow stronger through this difficulty?" Shifting your perspective empowers you to face challenges with optimism and resilience.

4. Expressing Gratitude:

Gratitude is not only felt but also expressed. Take the time to thank the people in your life who have made a positive impact.

Write a heartfelt note of appreciation, give a warm hug, or simply say "thank you" to those who have supported you. Expressing gratitude not only strengthens your relationships but also fills your heart with joy.

5. Gratitude in Adversity:

Practicing gratitude during difficult times may seem challenging, but it can be even more trans-formative.

During adversity, focus on the things that are still going well, no matter how small. Embrace the support and love you receive from others. Gratitude can be your anchor during storms, helping you navigate through even the darkest of times.

6. Cultivating a Grateful Heart:

Gratitude is a practice that can be cultivated over time. Incorporate gratitude into your daily routine by keeping a gratitude journal or setting reminders to pause and count your blessings.

As you continue to practice gratitude, you'll find that it becomes a natural part of your life, shaping your outlook and enriching your experiences.

7. Spreading the Attitude of Gratitude:

Gratitude is contagious, and when you practice it, you inspire others to do the same.

Share your gratitude with those around you, and encourage others to count their blessings. Spread the attitude of gratitude like a beautiful ripple effect, creating a more positive and grateful world.

Conclusion:

You've now discovered the transformative power of gratitude and how it allows you to focus on the positives in life.

Understand that gratitude is a way of life, and it starts with counting your blessings and shifting your perspective. Express your gratitude to others, especially during difficult times.

Cultivate a grateful heart by incorporating gratitude into your daily routine. Embrace gratitude as your anchor during challenges, helping you navigate through life's ups and downs with resilience and joy.

Share the attitude of gratitude with others, and watch as the world around you becomes brighter and more appreciative.

Onward to a life filled with gratitude and the power to see the beauty in every moment! You've got this, and your grateful heart is a beacon of light in the journey of life!

Chapter 16
Mastering Emotional Intelligence: Navigating through Ups and Downs

We'll explore the art of mastering emotional intelligence and how it empowers you to navigate through life's ups and downs with grace and understanding. Emotional intelligence is like a compass that guides you through the ever-changing seas of emotions. So, let's embark on this insightful journey of emotional intelligence, all in a friendly and compassionate tone.

1. Understanding Emotional Intelligence:

Emotional intelligence is the ability to recognize, understand, and manage both your own emotions and the emotions of others.

Recognize that emotions are a natural part of being human. Emotional intelligence empowers you to navigate through the vast ocean of emotions with greater self-awareness and empathy.

2. Cultivating Self-Awareness:

At the heart of emotional intelligence lies self-awareness. Take the time to connect with your emotions and understand their triggers.

Practice mindfulness and reflection to gain insights into your emotional patterns. Understanding your emotions allows you to respond more consciously and constructively to life's challenges.

3. Embracing Empathy:

Empathy is the bridge that connects us to others. Put yourself in someone else's shoes to understand their emotions and experiences.

When interacting with others, practice active listening and show genuine concern for their feelings. Empathy strengthens your relationships and fosters a supportive and compassionate community.

4. Managing Emotions:

Emotional intelligence equips you with the tools to manage your emotions effectively. Learn to express your emotions in a healthy and constructive manner.

Find healthy outlets for stress, such as exercise, journaling, or talking to a friend. Managing your emotions allows you to respond to challenges with a clear and level-headed approach.

5. Developing Social Skills:

Social skills are like sails that carry you through the sea of relationships. Practice effective communication and conflict resolution to strengthen your connections with others.

Be open to feedback and willing to collaborate with others. Developing social skills enhances your ability to navigate through the ups and downs of interpersonal dynamics.

6. Dealing with stress and resilience:

Emotional intelligence empowers you to handle stress and build resilience. Understand that stress is a part of life, but how you respond to it matters.

Practice self-care and prioritize your well-being during challenging times. Build resilience by embracing a growth mindset and learning from setbacks.

7. Practicing Emotional Intelligence in Daily Life:

Emotional intelligence is not just a concept; it's a skill that can be practiced in everyday life.

Pay attention to your emotions in various situations. Ask yourself, "How am I feeling right now?" or "How might others be feeling in this situation?" Use this awareness to respond with empathy and compassion.

Conclusion:

You've now discovered the art of mastering emotional intelligence and how it empowers you to navigate through life's ups and downs with grace and understanding.

Cultivate self-awareness to understand your emotions and triggers. Embrace empathy as a means of connecting with others and building compassionate relationships.

Learn to manage your emotions effectively and develop social skills for harmonious inter-actions. Handle stress with resilience, knowing that challenges are opportunities for growth.

Practice emotional intelligence in your daily life, allowing it to guide you through the ever-changing tides of emotions.

Onward to a life filled with emotional intelli-gence, compassion, and the ability to navigate through the highs and lows of life with grace and understanding! You've got this, and your emotionally intelligent heart is a beacon of light in the journey of emotions!

Chapter 17
Creating a Vision:
Charting the Course for Success

we'll explore the transformative process of creating a vision and how it empowers you to chart the course for success in your life. Just like a captain who sets sail with a clear destination in mind, having a vision provides you with a guiding star to navigate through life's vast ocean of possibilities. So, let's embark on this enlightening journey of vision creation, all in a friendly and inspiring tone.

1. Understanding the Power of Vision:

A vision is like a compass that guides you towards your dreams and aspirations. It's a clear picture of the future you want to create for yourself.

Understand that a vision is not just wishful thinking; it's a powerful tool that propels you into action and aligns your efforts with your goals.

2. Reflecting on Your Passions and Values:

Creating a vision starts with introspection. Reflect on your passions, interests, and core values.

Ask yourself, "What truly excites me?" or "What do I deeply care about?" Aligning your vision with your passions and values ensures that it resonates deeply with your soul.

3. Visualizing Your Ideal Future:

Close your eyes and let your imagination run wild. Visualize your ideal future in vivid detail.

Imagine every aspect of your life - personal, professional, and relationships. What does success look like to you? What do you want to achieve, and how do you want to impact the world around you?

4. Setting Specific Goals:

A vision without specific goals is like a ship without a destination. Break down your vision into actionable and achievable goals.

Set short-term and long-term goals that align with your vision. Each goal serves as a stepping stone towards the realization of your vision.

5. Embracing a Growth Mindset:

A growth mindset is the fuel that propels your vision into reality. Embrace the belief that you can develop your abilities through effort and learning.

Embrace challenges as opportunities for growth and see failures as valuable lessons. With a growth mindset, you'll approach your vision with resilience and determination.

6. Creating a Plan:

A vision without a plan is merely a wish. Create a detailed plan that outlines the steps required to achieve your goals.

Break your plan into manageable tasks and set deadlines to track your progress. A well-structured plan keeps you focused and on track towards success.

7. Overcoming Obstacles:

On your journey to realizing your vision, obstacles are inevitable. Embrace them as opportunities for learning and growth.

When faced with challenges, refer back to your vision and remember why you started this journey. Use your resilience and problem-solving skills to overcome roadblocks along the way.

8. Celebrating Milestones:

As you make progress towards your vision, celebrate every milestone you achieve.

Each milestone is a testament to your efforts and brings you closer to your ultimate goal.

Celebrate not only the big achievements but also the small wins that contribute to your success.

9. Revisiting and Revising Your Vision:

A vision is not set in stone; it can evolve as you grow and change. Periodically revisit your vision and assess whether it still aligns with your aspirations.

Be open to revising your vision if necessary, ensuring that it remains a reflection of your authentic desires and ambitions.

Conclusion:

You've now discovered the transformative power of creating a vision and how it empowers you to chart the course for success in your life.

Reflect on your passions and values to create a vision that resonates deeply with your soul. Visualize your ideal future and set specific goals to turn your vision into reality.

Embrace a growth mindset, create a detailed plan, and overcome obstacles with resilience. Celebrate every milestone you achieve, knowing that each step brings you closer to your dreams.

Periodically revisit and revise your vision to ensure it remains aligned with your aspirations. Your vision is the guiding star that illuminates your path to success.

Onward to a life filled with purpose, clarity, and the power to turn dreams into reality! You've got this, and your visionary heart is ready to set sail towards the bright horizons of success!

Chapter 18
The Art of Time Management: Maximizing Productivity

we'll dive into the art of time management and how it empowers you to make the most of your precious moments. Time is a precious resource, and managing it effectively is the key to achieving your goals and dreams. So, let's embark on this enriching journey of time management, all in a friendly and encouraging tone.

1. Understanding the Value of Time:

Time is a limited and non-renewable resource. Understanding the value of time is the first step in mastering time management.

Recognize that how you spend your time directly impacts the quality of your life and your ability to achieve your aspirations.

2. Identifying Your Priorities:

At the heart of time management lies identifying your priorities. Clarify your goals and determine the tasks and activities that align with them.

Ask yourself, "What are the most important things I need to accomplish?" Prioritizing your tasks ensures that you invest your time in what truly matters.

3. Creating a Schedule:

A well-structured schedule is like a roadmap that guides you through your day. Create a daily, weekly, or monthly schedule that allocates time to your various tasks and commitments.

Include time for work, personal activities, self-care, and relaxation. A schedule provides structure and helps you make the most of each day.

4. Setting Realistic Goals:

Setting ambitious but realistic goals is the cornerstone of effective time management. Break your goals down into smaller, achievable milestones.

Set deadlines for each milestone to track your progress. Realistic goals prevent overwhelm and keep you motivated on your journey.

5. Overcoming Procrastination:

Procrastination is the thief of time. Overcoming this habit is crucial in maximizing productivity.

Identify the reasons behind your procrastination and implement strategies to overcome it. Break tasks into smaller steps, create a conducive work environment, and use time-blocking techniques to stay focused.

6. Embracing Time-Blocking:

Time-blocking is a powerful technique that boosts productivity. Allocate specific blocks of time for specific tasks.

During each time block, focus solely on the designated task, free from distractions. Time-blocking helps you make significant progress on your priorities.

7. Learning to Say No:

Saying no is not selfish; it's essential for effective time management. Learn to decline tasks or commitments that don't align with your priorities.

Setting boundaries and saying no when necessary allows you to protect your time and energy for what truly matters.

8. Embracing Technology and Tools:

In the digital age, various time management tools and apps can streamline your efficiency.

Use productivity apps, calendars, and task management tools to organize your schedule and stay on track. Embracing technology enhances your time management capabilities.

9. Practicing Self-Care:

Taking care of yourself is fundamental to effective time management. Ensure you get enough rest, exercise, and nourishing food.

Schedule breaks and moments of relaxation to recharge your energy. Productivity is optimized when you are physically and mentally well.

10. Reflecting and Adjusting:

Time management is a continuous journey of improvement. Regularly reflect on your time management practices and assess what works and what can be improved.

Be flexible and adjust your strategies as needed. Embrace a growth mindset, recognizing that time management is a skill that can be refined over time.

Conclusion:

You've now discovered the art of time management and how it empowers you to maximize productivity and achieve your goals.

Understand the value of time and identify your priorities. Create a well-structured schedule and set realistic goals.

Overcome procrastination and embrace time-blocking to boost productivity. Learn to say no to tasks that don't align with your priorities.

Leverage technology and tools to enhance your time management capabilities. Prioritize self-care to maintain physical and mental well-being.

Regularly reflect on your time management practices and adjust as needed. With effective time management, you'll make the most of each moment and turn your dreams into reality.

Onward to a life filled with productivity, accomplishment, and the art of mastering time! You've got this, and your time management prowess will unlock the door to a more fulfilling and successful journey!

Chapter 19
Thriving in Adversity: Finding Joy Amidst Challenges

we'll explore the art of thriving in adversity and discovering joy amidst life's challenges. Adversity is an inevitable part of the human experience, but how we navigate through it can make all the difference. This chapter will be your guide to not just surviving but thriving in the face of adversity, all in a friendly and uplifting tone.

1. Embracing the Reality of Adversity:

Adversity is like a storm that may unexpectedly appear on our life's journey. Embrace the reality that challenges are a natural part of life, and you are not alone in facing them.

Recognize that it's okay to feel overwhelmed or discouraged, but also understand that adversity is an opportunity for growth and resilience.

2. Cultivating a Resilient Mindset:

Resilience is the anchor that helps you weather the storm of adversity. Cultivate a resilient mindset by acknowledging your emotions and finding healthy ways to cope.

Practice self-compassion and give yourself permission to feel vulnerable. Embrace the belief that you have the strength to rise above challenges and grow through them.

3. Finding Meaning in Adversity:

Adversity can be a catalyst for profound personal growth and self-discovery. Seek meaning in challenging situations and ask yourself, "What can I learn from this experience?"

Finding meaning in adversity can provide purpose and direction, helping you see challenges as stepping stones towards a more fulfilling life.

4. Focusing on what you can control:

Amidst adversity, it's essential to focus on what you can control rather than dwelling on what you cannot.

Identify the aspects of the situation where you can make a positive impact and take action. Redirecting your energy towards actionable steps empowers you to move forward.

5. Practicing Gratitude:

Gratitude is like a beacon of light that shines even in the darkest times. Practice gratitude by counting your blessings, no matter how small.

Focus on the positives in your life and express appreciation for the support you receive from loved ones. Gratitude uplifts your spirit and helps you find joy even in the face of challenges.

6. Seeking Support and Connection:

You don't have to navigate through adversity alone. Seek support from your friends, family, or a counselor.

Reach out to those who care about you and share your feelings. The power of human connection can provide solace and strength during difficult times.

7. Embracing Joyful Moments:

Amidst challenges, take time to embrace moments of joy and laughter. Engage in activities that bring you happiness, even if they provide temporary relief.

Allow yourself to experience joy without guilt, knowing that it nourishes your spirit and replenishes your resilience.

8. Practicing mindfulness:

Mindfulness is like an anchor that grounds you in the present moment. Engage in mindfulness practices such as meditation or deep breathing.

Being mindful helps you stay centered during adversity, allowing you to respond with clarity and calmness.

9. Celebrating Your Growth:

As you navigate through adversity and emerge stronger, celebrate your growth and progress.

Acknowledge the strength and resilience y-ou've shown in facing challenges. Each step forward, no matter how small, is a testament to your ability to thrive in adversity.

Conclusion:

You've now discovered the art of thriving in adversity and finding joy amidst life's challenges.

Embrace the reality of adversity and cultivate a resilient mindset. Find meaning in challenging situations and focus on what you can control.

Practice gratitude, seek support, and embrace moments of joy and connection. Engage in mindfulness to stay centered and respond with clarity.

Celebrate your growth and progress as you navigate through adversity. With resilience as your ally and joy as your companion, you'll not just survive but thrive through life's challenges.

Onward to a life filled with strength, joy, and the art of thriving in the face of adversity! You've got this, and your resilient spirit will shine brightly through the storms of life!

Chapter 20
Turning Passion into Purpose: Channeling Energy for Triumph

we'll explore the transformative journey of turning your passions into a driving purpose and how it empowers you to channel your energy for triumph. Passion and purpose are like two wings that enable you to soar to new heights of fulfillment and success. So, let's embark on this inspiring journey of turning your passions into purpose, all in a friendly and empowering tone.

1. Embracing the Power of Passion:

Passion is the fire that ignites your soul and fills your heart with enthusiasm. Embrace the things that genuinely excite you and bring you joy.

Recognize that passion is not limited to a specific activity or interest. It can be found in various aspects of your life, from hobbies to career aspirations.

2. Reflecting on Your Passions:

Take the time to reflect on your passions and understand why they hold such significance for you.

Ask yourself, "What activities make me lose track of time?" or "What brings me a sense of fulfillment?" Reflecting on your passions helps you discover your authentic desires.

3. Identifying the Connection to Purpose:

Turning passion into purpose involves understanding how your passions align with your values and the impact you want to make in the world.

Ask yourself, "How can I use my passions to serve others?" or "What positive change do I want to create?" Identifying the connection to purpose infuses your passions with meaning and direction.

4. Creating a Vision of Purpose:

Once you've identified the connection between your passions and purpose, create a clear vision of what living that purpose looks like.

Visualize yourself actively engaged in activities that align with your passions and purpose. Let this vision be your guiding light towards your triumph.

5. Taking Inspired Action:

A vision without action is merely a dream. Take inspired action to turn your vision of purpose into reality.

Break your vision down into actionable steps and set achievable goals. Each step forward, no matter how small, brings you closer to triumph.

6. Embracing Resilience:

On the journey of turning passion into purpose, challenges may arise, but resilience will carry you through.

Embrace resilience as you face setbacks and obstacles. Know that challenges are opportunities for growth and learning on the path to triumph.

7. Seeking Learning and Growth:

Continue to seek learning and growth on your journey. Invest in developing your skills and knowledge in areas related to your passions and purpose.

Read books, take courses, and seek mentorship to expand your understanding and expertise. Learning and growth fuel your journey towards triumph.

8. Embracing Gratitude and Joy:

As you channel your energy towards your purpose, embrace gratitude for the opportunity to live a life aligned with your passions.

Find joy in the process, celebrating each step you take towards your purpose. May gratitude and joy infuse your journey with positivity and fulfillment.

9. Inspiring Others:

As you embody your purpose, you become an inspiration to others. Share your journey with authenticity and vulnerability.

By living your purpose and following your passions, you encourage others to do the same. Your triumph becomes a beacon of hope for those seeking to find their own purpose.

Conclusion:

You've now discovered the transformative power of turning your passions into purpose and channeling your energy for triumph.

Embrace the power of passion and reflect on your authentic desires. Identify the connection between your passions and purpose, creating a clear vision of your triumph.

Take inspired action, embracing resilience as you navigate challenges. Seek learning and growth on your journey, and find gratitude and joy in the process.

Share your journey with others and become an inspiration for those seeking their purpose.

Onward to a life filled with purpose, passion, and the triumph of living your authentic truth! You've got this, and your passionate heart will guide you to remarkable heights of fulfillment and success!

Chapter 21
The Role of Mentorship:
Guiding and Being Guided

we'll explore the profound impact of mentorship and the transformative journey of both guiding and being guided. Mentorship is like a torch that illuminates the path of personal and professional growth, fostering a nurturing environment for knowledge exchange and support. So, let's embark on this enlightening journey of mentorship, all in a friendly and encouraging tone.

1. Understanding the Power of Mentorship:

Mentorship is a powerful relationship that goes beyond mere instruction; it's a bond built on trust, mutual respect, and shared growth.

Recognize that mentorship is not limited to formal arrangements. It can be found in various aspects of life, from academics and career to personal development.

2. Seeking Mentors:

As an eager learner, actively seek mentors who inspire you and align with your goals and values.

Look for individuals who possess the knowledge and experience you wish to gain. A mentor can provide guidance, share insights, and help you navigate challenges more effectively.

3. Cultivating Meaningful Connections:

Cultivating a meaningful mentor-mentee relationship involves open communication and genuine connection.

Engage in conversations with your mentor, expressing your aspirations, and seeking their advice. Be receptive to feedback and actively participate in your own growth.

4. Learning from experience:

A mentor's experiences can serve as invaluable life lessons. Learn from their triumphs and setbacks, embracing the wisdom they share.

Understand that learning from someone else's journey can save you time and help you make more informed decisions on your own path.

5. Embracing Vulnerability:

As a mentee, embrace vulnerability in your mentorship journey. Be honest about your challenges and fears, allowing your mentor to offer meaningful guidance.

Sharing your vulnerabilities fosters a deeper connection and allows your mentor to offer tailored support.

6. Being a mentor:

As you grow and gain experiences, consider becoming a mentor yourself.

Being a mentor is not about having all the answers; it's about providing support and guidance based on your own knowledge and experiences.

7. Nurturing the Mentor-Mentee Relationship:

In the role of a mentor, nurture the relationship with empathy and understanding.

Listen actively to your mentee's concerns and aspirations. Celebrate their successes and provide constructive feedback when needed.

8. Encouraging Growth and Independence:

A mentor's ultimate goal is to empower their mentee to stand on their own feet.

Encourage your mentee's growth and independence, allowing them to make their own decisions and learn from their experiences.

9. Creating a Supportive Community:

Mentorship is not limited to a one-on-one relationship. Encourage the creation of a supportive mentorship community.

Connect mentees with other like-minded individuals, fostering a network of support and knowledge exchange.

Conclusion:

You've now discovered the transformative power of mentorship and the remarkable journey of both guiding and being guided.

Understand the profound impact of mentorship and actively seek mentors who align with your goals.

Cultivate meaningful connections, embracing vulnerability as a mentee. Learn from your mentor's experiences and apply their wisdom to your own journey.

Consider becoming a mentor yourself, offering guidance and support to others.

Nurture the mentor-mentee relationship with empathy and celebrate growth and independence.

Encourage a supportive mentorship community, fostering knowledge exchange and mutual support.

Onward to a life filled with the transformative power of mentorship, where guidance and support pave the way for remarkable growth and shared success! You've got this, and your commitment to both guiding and being guided will lead to a thriving and enriching mentorship journey!

Chapter 22
Breaking Barriers:
Overcoming Limiting Beliefs

we'll explore the empowering journey of breaking barriers and overcoming limiting beliefs. Limiting beliefs are like invisible walls that hold us back from reaching our true potential. This chapter will be your guide to breaking free from these barriers, all in a friendly and supportive tone.

1. Understanding Limiting Beliefs:

Limiting beliefs are the negative thoughts and perceptions we hold about ourselves and our abilities. They often stem from past experiences or societal conditioning.

Recognize that these beliefs are not truths; they are simply perceptions that can be changed.

2. Identifying Your Limiting Beliefs:

Take the time to identify the specific limiting beliefs that are holding you back.

Ask yourself, "What do I believe about myself that might be hindering my growth?" or "What negative thoughts surface when I face challenges?" Being aware of your limiting beliefs is the first step towards overcoming them.

3. Challenging Your Beliefs:

Once you've identified your limiting beliefs, challenge their validity.

Ask yourself, "Is there concrete evidence to support this belief?" or "Have I allowed past failures to define my capabilities?" Often, you'll find that these beliefs lack substantial evidence and are based on fear rather than truth.

4. Embracing a Growth Mindset:

Embracing a growth mindset is a powerful tool for overcoming limiting beliefs.

Understand that your abilities and intelligence are not fixed; they can be developed with effort and learning. See challenges as opportunities for growth and view failures as stepping stones towards success.

5. Reframing Your Thoughts:

Reframing your thoughts is a technique that helps you replace limiting beliefs with empowering ones.

When a negative thought arises, challenge it and replace it with a positive affirmation. For example, if you think, "I'm not good enough," reframe it to, "I am capable, and I am continually improving."

6. Setting Realistic Goals:

Setting realistic goals is essential to building confidence and dispelling limiting beliefs.

Start with achievable goals that align with your passions and values. As you achieve these goals, your self-belief will grow, and you'll be more inclined to tackle bigger challenges.

7. Surrounding Yourself with Positivity:

Surround yourself with a positive and supportive environment.

Be mindful of the people you spend time with and the media you consume. Surrounding yourself with positivity uplifts your spirit and reinforces empowering beliefs.

8. Practicing Self-Compassion:

Be kind to yourself as you work through your limiting beliefs.

Acknowledge that everyone faces challenges and that it's okay to have moments of self-doubt. Treat yourself with the same compassion and encouragement you would offer a dear friend.

9. Celebrating Your Progress:

As you challenge and overcome your limiting beliefs, celebrate every step forward.

Acknowledge your growth and the courage it takes to face your barriers. Celebrating your progress reinforces your newfound confidence and determination.

Conclusion:

You've now discovered the empowering journey of breaking barriers and overcoming limiting beliefs.

Understand that limiting beliefs are perceptions that can be changed. Identify your limiting beliefs and challenge their validity.

Embrace a growth mindset, reframing negative thoughts, and setting realistic goals. Surround yourself with positivity and practice self-compassion.

Celebrate your progress, knowing that each step forward dismantles the barriers that once held you back.

Onward to a life free from limiting beliefs, where courage and self-belief open doors to infinite possibilities! You've got this, and your determination to break barriers will lead you to a future filled with growth and success!

Chapter 23
The Science of Stress Management: Balancing Mental Well-being

we'll delve into the science of stress management and the art of balancing your mental well-being. Stress is a natural response to life's challenges, but how we manage it can significantly impact our overall health and happiness. This chapter will be your guide to understanding and mastering stress management, all in a friendly and compassionate tone.

1. Understanding Stress and Its Impact:

Stress is your body's response to perceived threats or demands. While some stress can be motivating, chronic stress can negatively impact your mental and physical health.

Recognize the signs of stress, such as increased irritability, difficulty sleeping, and physical tension. Understanding stress and its impact is the first step towards effective management.

2. Identifying Stress Triggers:

Identify the specific situations or events that trigger stress in your life.

Ask yourself, "What situations make me feel overwhelmed?" or "What responsibilities or commitments add the most pressure?" Recognizing stress triggers helps you devise targeted coping strategies.

3. Practicing Mindfulness and Relaxation Techniques:

Mindfulness and relaxation techniques are powerful tools for managing stress.

Practice meditation, deep breathing, or progressive muscle relaxation to calm your mind and body. Mindfulness allows you to be present in the moment, reducing anxiety about the past or future.

4. Developing Healthy Coping Mechanisms:

Healthy coping mechanisms are essential for managing stress in a positive way.

Engage in activities that bring you joy and relaxation, such as hobbies, exercise, or spending time in nature. Avoid turning to unhealthy habits, such as excessive alcohol consumption or emotional eating, to cope with stress.

5. Building Resilience:

Resilience is the ability to bounce back from adversity. Strengthen your resilience to handle stress more effectively.

Focus on building a strong support network, seeking help when needed, and reframing challenges as opportunities for growth. Resilience empowers you to face stress with a positive mindset.

6. Prioritizing Self-Care:

Self-care is a crucial aspect of stress management and mental well-being.

Prioritize self-care activities that nurture your mind, body, and soul. Get enough sleep, maintain a balanced diet, and engage in activities that bring you joy and relaxation.

7. Setting Boundaries:

Setting boundaries is essential for managing stress and preventing burnout.

Learn to say no to additional commitments that exceed your capacity. Establishing boundaries allows you to protect your time and energy, promoting mental well-being.

8. Seeking Professional Support:

If stress becomes overwhelming or persistent, don't hesitate to seek professional support.

Consult a mental health professional or counselor to explore stress management strategies tailored to your specific needs. Seeking help is a sign of strength, not weakness.

9. Reflecting and Adapting:

Stress management is an ongoing process of reflection and adaptation.

Regularly assess your stress levels and coping strategies. Be open to adjusting your approach to find what works best for you.

Conclusion:

You've now discovered the science of stress management and the art of balancing your mental well-being.

Understand stress and its impact, identifying your stress triggers. Practice mindfulness and relaxation techniques to cultivate inner peace.

Develop healthy coping mechanisms, building resilience to face challenges with strength and positivity.

Prioritize self-care, set boundaries, and seek professional support when needed. Reflect on your stress management strategies and adapt them to meet your evolving needs.

Onward to a life filled with balance, resilience, and the mastery of stress management! You've got this, and your commitment to nurturing your mental well-being will lead you to a future of peace and serenity!

Chapter 24
Embracing Change:
The Gateway to New Opportunities

we'll explore the empowering journey of embracing change and the endless opportunities it brings into your life. Change is a natural and constant part of our existence, and how we navigate it can shape our growth and success. This chapter will be your guide to embracing change with open arms, all in a friendly and encouraging tone.

1. Understanding the Nature of Change:

Change is an inherent part of life, and it can manifest in various forms - personal, professional, or circumstantial.

Recognize that change is not to be feared but embraced as an avenue for growth and transformation.

2. Embracing a Growth Mindset:

A growth mindset is the key to embracing change with a positive outlook.

Believe that you have the capacity to learn, adapt, and improve. Embrace challenges as opportunities for growth rather than as obstacles.

3. Recognizing the Benefits of Change:

Change opens the door to new possibilities and experiences.

Ask yourself, "What positive outcomes can arise from this change?" or "How can this change lead to personal or professional growth?" Recognizing the benefits of change motivates you to embrace it willingly.

4. Letting Go of the Familiar:

Embracing change often requires letting go of the familiar and stepping into the unknown.

Be willing to release attachments to old habits, routines, or beliefs that no longer serve you. Embrace the uncertainty with the anticipation of new opportunities ahead.

5. Setting Goals for the New Chapter:

Change provides a blank canvas for you to set new goals and aspirations.

Take time to define your vision for this new chapter. What do you want to achieve or experience during this time of change? Setting goals provides direction and purpose.

6. Finding Support in Change:

Change can be easier to navigate with a support system.

Share your thoughts and feelings with trusted friends, family, or colleagues. Seek support from those who have experienced similar changes or can offer guidance.

7. Taking Small Steps:

Embracing change does not mean taking giant leaps; Progress can be made with small
steps.

Break down your goals into manageable tasks
and take one step at a time. Celebrate each small
achievement, knowing that they accumulate to
create significant change.

8. Practicing Self-Compassion:

Change can be challenging, and it's essential
to practice self-compassion throughout the
process.

Be gentle with yourself as you adapt to the
new circumstances. Treat yourself with kindness and understanding, just as you would treat
a dear friend.

9. Celebrating the Journey:

Embracing change is a journey filled with
growth and self-discovery.

Celebrate your progress, resilience, and willingness to embrace change. Acknowledge that every step forward is an accomplishment that brings you closer to new opportunities.

Conclusion:

You've now discovered the empowering journey of embracing change and welcoming new opportunities into your life.

Understand that change is a constant in life and embrace it as a gateway to growth.

Cultivate a growth mindset, recognize the benefits of change and letting go of the familiar.

Set goals for the new chapter, find support, and take small steps towards progress.

Practice self-compassion throughout the process and celebrate each milestone on your journey of change.

Onward to a life filled with openness, growth, and the power of embracing change! You've got this, and your willingness to adapt will lead you to a future brimming with endless possibilities!

Chapter 25
Living with Intention:
Directing Efforts toward Success

we'll explore the transformative journey of living with intention and directing your efforts toward success. Living with intention means a-ligning your actions with your values and goals, and it's a powerful way to create a life of purpose and fulfillment. This chapter will be your guide to embracing intentionality, all in a friendly and empowering tone.

1. Understanding Living with Intention:

Living with intention means being mindful of your choices and actions, ensuring they align with your values and aspirations.

Recognize that living with intention is about taking control of your life's direction, rather than being passively carried along by external circumstances.

2. Clarifying Your Values and Goals:

Begin your journey of living with intention by clarifying your core values and setting meaningful goals.

Ask yourself, "What truly matters to me?" and "What do I want to achieve in life?" Understanding your values and goals provides a compass for intentional living.

3. Creating a Personal Mission Statement:

Craft a personal mission statement that reflects your values, purpose, and aspirations.

Your mission statement serves as a guiding mantra, reminding you of your intentions and motivating you to stay focused on what matters most.

4. Align Daily Actions with Intentions:

Living with intention involves aligning your daily actions with your values and goals.

Ask yourself each day, "How can I take a step closer to my goals today?" and "How can I live in harmony with my values?" Be mindful of your choices to ensure they reflect your intentions.

5. Eliminating Distractions:

Intentional living requires eliminating distractions that derail you from your path.

Identify distractions that consume your time and energy, and take steps to reduce or eliminate them. Create an environment that supports your focused efforts.

6. Practicing Mindfulness in Everyday Life:

Mindfulness is an essential practice for living with intention.

Engage in daily mindfulness exercises, such as meditation or mindful breathing. Being present in the moment helps you make conscious decisions aligned with your intentions.

7. Embracing Gratitude:

Cultivate a grateful heart as you live with intention.

Regularly express gratitude for the opportunities and experiences that align with your values and goals. Gratitude nurtures a positive mindset and reinforces intentional living.

8. Learning from Challenges:

Embrace challenges as opportunities for growth and learning.

When faced with obstacles, ask yourself, "How can I overcome this challenge while staying true to my intentions?" Use challenges as stepping stones on your intentional journey.

9. Celebrating Your Progress:

Living with intention is a continuous journey of growth and achievement.

Celebrate your progress and accomplishments, no matter how small. Acknowledge the efforts you put into aligning your life with your intentions.

Conclusion:

You've now discovered the transformative power of living with intention and directing your efforts towards success.

Understand that living with intention is about aligning your actions with your values and goals.

Clarify your values and set meaningful goals, creating a personal mission statement as your guiding mantra.

Align your daily actions with your intentions and eliminate distractions that hinder your progress.

Practice mindfulness and gratitude in every-day life, embracing challenges as opportunities for growth.

Celebrate your progress on your intentional journey, knowing that each step forward brings you closer to a life of purpose and fulfillment.

Onward to a life filled with intention, focus, and the power to direct your efforts towards success! You've got this, and your commitment to living with purpose will lead you to a future of remarkable achievements and deep fulfillment!

Chapter 26
Triumph in Relationships: Building Bonds that Empower

we'll explore the profound impact of building empowering relationships and the transformative journey of triumph in human connections. Relationships are the cornerstone of our lives, and fostering bonds that empower us can lead to incredible personal growth and fulfillment. This chapter will be your guide to creating meaningful relationships, all in a friendly and supportive tone.

1. Understanding the Power of Relationships:

Relationships form the fabric of our lives, influencing our emotions, well-being, and overall happiness.

Recognize that nurturing empowering relationships is a reciprocal process, where both parties contribute to each other's growth and success.

2. Honoring Authenticity:

Embrace authenticity as the foundation of empowering relationships.

Be genuine in your interactions, expressing your thoughts, feelings, and values openly. Honoring authenticity creates trust and fosters a deeper connection.

3. Active Listening and Empathy:

Practice active listening and empathy to understand others on a deeper level.

Give your full attention to those you interact with, truly hearing their words and emotions. Empathize with their experiences, acknowledging their feelings without judgment.

4. Communication as a Bridge:

Communication is the bridge that connects us in relationships.

Strive for clear and compassionate communication, expressing yourself honestly while respecting others' perspectives. Effective communication deepens understanding and resolves conflicts constructively.

5. Supporting Each Other's Growth:

Empowering relationships support each other's personal growth and aspirations.

Encourage and celebrate each other's achievements and be a source of strength during challenges. Be a cheerleader for each other's dreams and aspirations.

6. Resolving conflicts with respect:

Conflicts are natural in any relationship, but how we handle them matters.

Approach conflicts with respect and a willingness to understand the other person's point of view. Seek resolution through compromise and find common ground.

7. Setting Healthy Boundaries:

Healthy boundaries are essential for maintaining empowering relationships.

Communicate your needs and establish boundaries that protect your well-being. Respect others' boundaries, fostering an environment of mutual respect and trust.

8. Practicing Gratitude:

Gratitude is a powerful way to nurture empowering relationships.

Express gratitude for the presence and impact of others in your life. Regularly acknowledge the positive contributions they make to your journey.

9. Embracing Vulnerability:

Vulnerability deepens connections in empowering relationships.

Share your hopes, fears, and challenges with trusted individuals. Embracing vulnerability fosters intimacy and strengthens the bond between you.

10. Celebrating Togetherness:

Celebrate the joy of togetherness in empowering relationships.

Create opportunities for shared experiences and meaningful moments. Celebrate milestones and accomplishments as a testament to the power of your bond.

Conclusion:

You've now discovered the transformative power of building empowering relationships and the joy of triumph in human connections.

Understand that relationships are the fabric of our lives, influencing our growth and happiness.

Honor authenticity and practice active listening and empathy. Communicate with clarity and compassion, supporting each other's growth and aspirations.

Resolve conflicts with respect and set healthy boundaries to maintain mutual respect and trust.

Practice gratitude and embrace vulnerability to deepen connections. Celebrate the joy of togetherness as a testament to the power of your bond.

Onward to a life filled with empowering relationships, where your compassionate heart enriches the lives of those around you! You've got this, and your commitment to building bonds that empower will lead you to a future of deep fulfillment and meaningful connections!

Chapter 27
Celebrating Milestones: Acknowledging Achievements Along the Way

we'll explore the uplifting journey of celebrating milestones and the profound impact of acknowledging achievements along your path. Life is a series of stepping stones, and each milestone reached deserves recognition and celebration. This chapter will be your guide to embracing the art of celebration, all in a friendly and encouraging tone.

1. The Importance of Celebrating Milestones:

Celebrating milestones is more than just reveling in accomplishments; it's a way to honor your progress and boost your motivation.

Recognize that celebrating milestones is an opportunity to reflect on how far you've come and acknowledge the effort you've put into your journey.

2. Setting Meaningful Milestones:

Set meaningful milestones along your path to success.

Break your larger goals into smaller, achievable steps. Each milestone should mark significant progress toward your ultimate vision.

3. Embracing Small Victories:

Don't underestimate the power of small victories.

Acknowledge and celebrate even the smallest wins. They are stepping stones that keep you moving forward with positivity.

4. Creating Personal Rewards:

Create personal rewards for reaching milestones.

Treat yourself to something that brings joy and aligns with your values. Personal rewards serve as positive reinforcement for your efforts.

5. Sharing Your Success:

Share your achievements with others who have supported you on your journey.

Allow yourself to bask in the well-wishes and congratulations of friends, family, and colleagues. Their encouragement strengthens your sense of accomplishment.

6. Reflecting on Overcoming Challenges:

As you celebrate milestones, reflect on the challenges you've overcome.

Acknowledge the obstacles you faced and the resilience you demonstrated. Celebrating milestones is also about recognizing your capacity to overcome adversity.

7. Gratitude for Progress:

Practice gratitude for the progress you've made.

Be thankful for the opportunities, experiences, and people that have contributed to your success. Gratitude amplifies the joy of celebration.

8. Setting New Goals:

Use milestones as opportunities to set new goals.

After celebrating a milestone, take time to reassess and set new objectives. This keeps you focused and motivated to continue growing.

9. Spreading Positivity:

Spread positivity by acknowledging and celebrating the achievements of others.

Celebrate the successes of friends, family, or colleagues with genuine joy. Celebrating others creates a supportive and uplifting community.

10. Cultivating a Celebration Mindset:

Embrace a celebration mindset as part of your journey.

Look for reasons to celebrate, even in everyday accomplishments. A celebration mindset infuses your life with joy and appreciation.

Conclusion:

You've now discovered the uplifting journey of celebrating milestones and the profound impact of acknowledging achievements along your path.

Understand that celebrating milestones is a way to honor your progress and boost your motivation.

Set meaningful milestones, embracing small victories along the way. Create personal rewards and share your success with others.

Reflect on challenges overcome and practice gratitude for your progress. Set new goals after each milestone and spread positivity by celebrating the achievements of others.

Embrace a celebration mindset as an integral part of your journey, infusing your life with joy and appreciation.

Onward to a life filled with celebration, gratitude, and the joy of acknowledging your achievements along the way! You've achieved this, and your commitment to celebrating milestones will lead you to a future of continued growth and remarkable accomplishments!

Chapter 28
The Journey Continues: Sustaining Triumph and Inspiring Others

we'll explore the inspiring journey of sustaining triumph and the profound impact of using your success to inspire others. Triumph is not a singular event; it's a continual process of growth and learning. This chapter will be your guide to sustaining your achievements and uplifting those around you, all in a friendly and empowering tone.

1. Embracing the Journey of Triumph:

Understand that triumph is not an endpoint; it's a journey of ongoing growth and progress.

Embrace the mindset that every milestone is an opportunity to build upon your success and continue to evolve.

2. Reflecting on Your Triumphs:

Take time to reflect on your triumphs and the path you've traveled.

Acknowledge the hard work, dedication, and resilience that led you to your achievements. Reflecting on your triumphs reinforces your motivation to keep going.

3. Setting New Goals and Challenges:

Sustaining triumph involves setting new goals and challenges.

Continually strive for personal and professional growth by identifying new aspirations and opportunities. Setting fresh objectives keeps your journey dynamic and exciting.

4. Empowering Others with Your Story:

Share your triumphs and the lessons you've learned with others.

Your story can inspire and empower those who are on their own paths. Be open about your challenges and how you overcame them, offering guidance to those who may face similar obstacles.

5. Becoming a Mentor:

Consider becoming a mentor to others who seek guidance.

Your triumphs have equipped you with valuable experiences to share. Being a mentor can be a rewarding way to give back and positively impact someone else's journey.

6. Supporting Others' Triumphs:

Be a source of support and celebration for others' triumphs.

Cheer on your friends, family, or colleagues as they achieve their goals. Celebrating others' success fosters a sense of camaraderie and creates a positive and encouraging community.

7. Cultivating Resilience:

Sustaining triumph requires resilience in the face of challenges.

View setbacks as opportunities to learn and grow. Cultivate the ability to bounce back stronger after adversity.

8. Practicing Gratitude:

Practice gratitude for the journey and the people who have contributed to your triumphs.

Express appreciation for the support and opportunities that have played a role in your success. Gratitude nurtures a humble and compassionate spirit.

9. Embracing Lifelong Learning:

Stay curious and embrace lifelong learning as you sustain your triumphs.

Continuously seek new knowledge and skills to stay relevant and adaptable. Learning keeps your journey vibrant and enriching.

10. Celebrating the Progress of Others:

Celebrate the progress of others with genuine joy and encouragement.

Acknowledge the efforts and achievements of those around you, fostering a culture of support and inspiration.

Conclusion:

You've now discovered the inspiring journey of sustaining triumph and using your success to uplift others.

Understand that triumph is a continuous process of growth and learning.

Reflect on your triumphs, setting new goals and challenges to keep your journey dynamic.

Empower others with your story, becoming a mentor to offer guidance and support.

Celebrate others' triumphs and be a source of encouragement for their journey.

Cultivate resilience, practice gratitude, and embrace lifelong learning.

Onward to a life of sustained triumph, where your inspiring journey motivates others to reach for their own greatness! You've got this, and your commitment to uplifting those around you will lead you to a future of continued success and positive impact!

The Secret a rich life and how to play it
© by 2023 Russom Teklay
Manufacturing and Publishing: D2D

Milton Keynes UK
Ingram Content Group UK Ltd.
UKHW020250221123
432980UK00016B/844